GLENN MCGRATH COLOR

AUSTRALIAN CRICKETER

MR VIVEK KUMAR PANDEY SHAMBHUNATH

Copyright © Mr Vivek Kumar Pandey Shambhunath
All Rights Reserved.

ISBN 979-888555631-6

This book has been published with all efforts taken to make the material error-free after the consent of the author. However, the author and the publisher do not assume and hereby disclaim any liability to any party for any loss, damage, or disruption caused by errors or omissions, whether such errors or omissions result from negligence, accident, or any other cause.

While every effort has been made to avoid any mistake or omission, this publication is being sold on the condition and understanding that neither the author nor the publishers or printers would be liable in any manner to any person by reason of any mistake or omission in this publication or for any action taken or omitted to be taken or advice rendered or accepted on the basis of this work. For any defect in printing or binding the publishers will be liable only to replace the defective copy by another copy of this work then available.

Disclaimer : During Writing This Book No character & No religious , No Relation Members Are Harmed. It's Only For Study & Entertainment Purpose. Do Not Take Seriously. Short Biopic Written In This Book Written By Mr Vivek Kumar Pandey.

Contents

Foreword

Short biography of Glenn McGrath and about life.During writing this book no character & no religious are harmed written by Mr Vivek Kumar Pandey. winner youngest writer award 1st rank in india 2020.He is only one writer can publish 790+ own book that was greatest successfull in his life.This All Credit Goes To My Super Hero Daddy. This book fully colour Edition.

Preface

Author biography in English :MY NAME IS VIVEK KUMAR PANDEY . I WAS BORN IN 30 SEP 2002,I AM FROM SURAT GUJARAT INDIA.MY DREAM WAS TO BE GOOD WRITERS ,MY FAMILY SUPPORTED ME TO SUCCESSFUL AND I CAN DO IT MY SELF.How do I write? That is a question, I believe, that can be honestly answered by me."CELEBRATING YOUNGEST WRITER AWARD WINNER IN GUJARAT 1ST RANK" MR PANDEY JI . I may think I did a good job writing something . The reader is the one who decides the quality of my writing. I do find writing to be natural to me and therefore find it to be a real challenge. My trick as a challenged writer is to do the best I can and know that I am happy with the final outcome. It may take a while to do my best and there may be quite a few problems I run into along the way.

I am not a greedy person those who are thinking about me and my self I never tried it anyone people suffering from sadness ,I trying to get promoted people suffering from happiness and joy in your Life Time. Now in current situation in India and also world people are unemployed and have no many but our indian governor help to people to get free food from ration card , i also take part in leadership team ,i am Motivational speaker , Film script writer. There was my two dream firstly writer and secondly actor & also my own film is upcoming soon i done almost completely completed script for my film .I AM GOING TO SAY WORD OF HEART TOUCH OUT PLEASE READ IT" , firstly i thanks my father he supports me in this field they always getting inspired me by own his words and behavior ,they always said that he was a biggest person in the world in future and also they purchase fruit and chocolate for me in anytime & anyway , firstly my father buy him then call me Vivek you want a chocolate i will say yes papa but how many tell me ,papa: you tell me how much i buy him i told 1 or 2 chocolate but my father purchase whole the boxes of chocolate and they get suprised me. MY FATHER WAS BORN IN " 20 SEPTEMBER" 1971 IN INDIA.

1) MY FATHER FAVORITE CLOTHES IS KURTA PAIJMA AND ALSO STYLES SHOE

2) FAVORITE SINGER IS KISHORE DA

3) FAVORITE STATE GUJARAT AND KOLKATA , HIS VILLAGE IN BIHAR

4) FAVORITE COLOR BLACK AND WHITE

THEY ALSO LOVE cricket like IPL and one day t-20 .they also like watching a News daily and heard the song daily ,they also interested in tik tok video but in current time tik tok is banned in india but also few videos are in you tube. In lockdown time my family and me very enjoy day daily. my father play daily ludo with his sister and son, daughter.they always loved tea and coffee anytime call me "। विवेक थोड़ा चाय बनाओना विवेक तुम्हारे हाथ का चाय अच्छा लगता है". I make it tea for my father but some reason after the April to june they are suffering from fever and cough , weakness on 6 June 2020 my father death. they not told me say bye bye his life. After death of 6 June on 10 june my mom and dad anniversary.but my father is Best in the world they can do anything for me please take care of father and respect it of your parents.

CHAPTER ONE

Glenn McGrath Color

- Glenn McGrath Color

1. Disclaimer : During Writing This Book No character & No religious , No Relation Members Are Harmed. It's Only For Study & Entertainment Purpose. Do Not Take Seriously. Short Biopic Written In This Book Written By Mr Vivek Kumar Pandey.

Glenn Donald McGrath born 9 February 1970 is an Australian former international cricketer who played international cricket for 14 years. He was a fast-medium pace bowler and is considered one of the greatest Australian international bowlers of all time, and a leading contributor to Australia's domination of world cricket from the mid-1990s to the late-2000s.

Known throughout his career for maintaining an accurate line and length, McGrath displayed a consistency that enabled him to be one of the most economical and successful fast bowlers of his time. In terms of total career wickets taken by fast bowlers, McGrath is the second most successful of all time behind James Anderson. On the list of all bowlers, he is fifth. He has also taken the seventh-highest number of one day international wickets (381) and holds the record for most wickets (71) in the Cricket World Cup.

McGrath announced his retirement from Test cricket on 23 December 2006, with his Test career coming to an end after the fifth Ashes Test in Sydney in January 2007, while the 2007 World Cup, which marked the end of his one-day career, saw him win the man-of-the-tournament award for his outstanding bowling, which was instrumental in Australia winning the tournament.

McGrath later played for the Indian Premier League team of the Delhi DareDevils and was one of the competition's most economical bowlers during its first season, but he saw no action in the second season, ultimately having his contract bought out.

McGrath is the director of MRF Pace Foundation, Chennai, replacing Dennis Lillee, who served for 25 years. He currently serves as president of the McGrath Foundation, a breast cancer support and education charity he founded with his late first wife, Jane.McGrath was honoured during the seventh annual Bradman Awards in Sydney on 1 November 2012. He was inducted into the ICC Hall of fame in January 2013.

- Glenn McGrath Early year

McGrath was born in Dubbo to Beverly and Kevin McGrath. He grew up in Narromine, New South Wales (NSW), where he first played cricket, and his potential was spotted by Doug Walters. He moved to Sydney to play grade cricket for Sutherland and made his debut for NSW during the 1992–93 season. McGrath capped his rapid rise in the next Australian summer with selection in the Test team after only eight first-class matches.

McGrath's Test debut was against New Zealand at Perth in 1993–1994. In Australia's 1995 Test series victory McGrath took the approach of bouncing the West Indies team, including the bowlers, which had not happened before. In McGrath's biography, Ricky Ponting is quoted as saying:

I remember thinking Glenn's decision to take on the West Indies bowlers sent out a positive message to the West Indies that the Australian side was really up for it. Ambrose, Walsh, Kenny Benjamin had never been treated like that before. It made the West Indies sit back and think, 'This Australian team is fair dinkum—they're really up for it.' Even if you aren't the murder boys of cricket, you can show little things to let the opposition know you are serious. It might be the way you warm up, how you dress to go to the ground. Perception can be enormous. If you can give off the right signals to (a) bluffing them or (b) showing them what you're all about. McGrath, at that stage of his career, showed them what he was all about. His body language and the way he looked at their batsman — the wry smile — it sent a signal to the batsman and his own team-mates that he knew what he was doing.

- Glenn McGrath County cricket in England

McGrath played for Worcestershire in the 2000 English County Championship, proving both successful on the field and popular with the county's supporters. In 14 first-class games he took 80 wickets at 13.21, including an outstanding innings return of 8–41 against Northamptonshire, as well as making his first-ever first-class half-century (55 against Nottinghamshire). He also played a few games for Middlesex in 2004; although accurate, he could manage only nine wickets in four first-class appearances for the county.

- Glenn McGrath Against England (Ashes 2005 and 2006/07)

During the first Test at Lord's in the 2005 Ashes series McGrath became the fourth bowler in history to take 500 Test wickets with the dismissal of Marcus Trescothick. This wicket was also the start of a productive spell of 5–2 that led to England being bowled out for 155. McGrath took 4–29 in the second innings and was named man of the match in a comprehensive Australian victory.

- McGrath at a Test match at the SCG in 2007

McGrath trod on a cricket ball and injured his ankle the morning before the start of the second Test at Edgbaston and was unable to play in the match, in which England amassed 407 runs in one day against the McGrath-less bowling attack to win by two runs. He was rushed back when not fully fit for the third Test at Old Trafford, where he earned another five-wicket haul in the second innings of a drawn game, batting in a last-wicket partnership with Brett Lee in the last hour of the Test to deny an English victory.

He then missed the fourth Test at Trent Bridge, which England won by three wickets, with an elbow injury. McGrath returned for the final Test at The Oval but he and the rest of the Australian team were unable to force a result and the match was drawn, giving England the series win. McGrath's injury problems are seen as a key factor in England regaining the Ashes, as their victories came in matches in which he was absent.

Australia hosted England in the 2006-07 Ashes series and regained the Ashes, beating England 5–0, only the second 5–0 series whitewash in Ashes history (the first time was by the Australian team during the 1920–1921 Ashes Series, and the later 2013–14 Ashes series). Having taken a break from cricket since April 2006, McGrath used the 2006 ICC Champions Trophy to reclaim his spot in Australia's Test XI. He took a six-wicket haul in his comeback innings in the first test at the Gabba to set the tone for the rest of the series, with Australia winning back the Ashes in a record-breaking 15 days of play. McGrath took 21 wickets in the series at an average of 23.90, and scored 10 runs and took a catch in what would be his final test series.

- In his biography McGrath wrote

There was an incredible sense of emotion and elation as I walked around the Sydney Cricket Ground with my team-mates, holding hands with my children, James and Holly. I didn't feel the slightest sense of sadness about retiring. I knew I'd reached the end; my body told me that. And even more importantly, I'd realised that those special moments I was missing in the life and times of my family were too great ... the moments had become weeks at a time, and I didn't like it.

- Glenn McGrath Retirement

McGrath in his final test series – the 2006-07 Ashes series

On 23 December 2006, McGrath announced his retirement from Tests. His last Test was the fifth Ashes Test against England in Sydney in January 2007, where he took a wicket with the last ball of his Test career. He retired from all forms of international cricket following the successful 2007 Cricket World Cup, at which he became the leading wicket taker in the history of the World Cup, while also being the tournament's top wicket taker with 26 and being named player of the tournament. He was named in the 'Team of the Tournament' by ESPNCricinfo for the 2007 World Cup. His spell of 3-18 against South Africa was named as the fifth-best ODI bowling performance of the year by ESPNCricinfo voters.

Indian Premier League

McGrath was signed by the Delhi DareDevils for the 2008 Indian Premier League, the first season of the Indian Premier League. He played in 14 matches for the side and was the team's most economic bowler during the competition. He was resigned for the 2009 competition but did not play a match. After playing twice for Delhi in the 2009 Champions League Twenty20, in January 2010 the franchise announced that it had bought out the remaining year of McGrath's contract, effectively bringing his cricketing career to an end.

- Glenn McGrath Playing style

McGrath's bowling was not of express pace. Rather, he relied on unerring accuracy and subtle seam movement, which he derived from his high wrist action and lengthy follow-through. His height (195 cm), combined with a high arm action, allowed him to extract extra bounce, which often surprised batsmen. In the later years of his career he developed as a swing bowler.

His uncomplicated method and natural physical fitness were significant factors in the longevity of McGrath's career. In 2004, he became the first Australian fast bowler to play 100 Tests. In the first innings of the ICC Super Series Test match in 2005, McGrath passed Courtney Walsh to become the greatest wicket-taker among fast bowlers in Test history.

McGrath was regarded as one of the best fast bowlers in the world and has had success against every opposition team, in both Test and one-day cricket. He deliberately (and publicly) targeted the opposition's best batsmen prior to a series in an attempt to distract them, a ploy that regularly worked. At the beginning of the Frank Worrell series against the West Indies he stated in interviews before the match that he would dismiss Sherwin Campbell for his 299th wicket, then remove star batsman Brian Lara for his 300th wicket the very next ball.

This happened as planned, and he followed this with the dismissal of captain Jimmy Adams to complete a memorable hat-trick. The targeting of opposition batsmen was generally successful; he dismissed Mike Atherton of England 19 times – the most times any batsman has been dismissed by one bowler in cricket history. On the other hand, he targeted Michael Vaughan prior to the 2002/03 Ashes series in Australia, with Vaughan going on to score three centuries at an average greater than 60. He targeted Andrew Strauss in the 2005 series in England, who went on to score two centuries.

He also tended to engage in sledging of opposition batsmen and teams, though it didn't always pay off. Before the 2005 Ashes series he predicted a 5–0 whitewash for Australia, and even said that if England won the Ashes he would return to Australia by boat, but England prevailed 2–1. However, this did not dissuade him from making a similar 5–0 prediction for the next Ashes series, in Australia in 2006/07, which turned out to be true. He finished his career as the most successful Test fast bowler and third-highest Test wicket taker.

- Glenn McGrath Fielding

McGrath was not known as a competent outfielder but he had a strong and accurate throwing arm; while not known for his athleticism, he took an exceptional outfield catch on one memorable occasion in 2002 at the Adelaide Oval against England, dismissing English batsman Michael Vaughan from the bowling of Shane Warne, running many metres before leaping into the air and catching the ball with arms outstretched and body horizontal. His captain, Steve Waugh, described the famous catch as "a miracle" and "one of the great catches in history".

- Glenn McGrath Batting

Mark Taylor: Average of 6.5 from McGrath and that has grown throughout his career. It was sub 2 at one stage.I an Healy: Langer [is] very bored reading a book, Gilchrist getting ready to keep. The rest [have] not much faith in McGrath and Gillespie and their partnership.Mark Taylor and Ian Healy commentary in the opening stages of McGrath's career best 61 run innings.

McGrath's batting prowess, in the early phases of his career, was poor; in fact, he scored first-ball ducks (zero runs) on both his Test and One-Day International debuts, and his batting average hovered below 4 for the first few years of his career. Years of patient tutelage from captain and friend Steve Waugh improved this aspect of his game to the point where he scored a Test half-century, which came on 20 November 2004 against New Zealand Full Scorecard of Australia vs New Zealand 1st Test 2004 - Score Report | ESPNcricinfo.com at the Gabba. His final score in that innings was 61, sharing a last wicket stand of 114 with Jason Gillespie (54*) to hilarity and the acclaim of their team-mates.

Nevertheless, McGrath was, for the duration of his career, regarded as a batting 'bunny', although he pushed his average above 7.00 runs/dismissal by the end of his career. In the first World Cricket Tsunami Appeal charity match, he was promoted to bat at number 6 ahead of specialist batsmen Stephen Fleming and Matthew Hayden, but was dismissed first ball trying to slog Muttiah Muralitharan. Towards the end of his international career McGrath, while not scoring many runs himself, became rather more difficult for opposing bowlers to dismiss, being dismissed only once during the 2005 Ashes series. With a contribution of 11 runs in the first innings of the MCG 2005 Boxing Day Test versus South Africa Full Scorecard of Australia vs South Africa 2nd Test 2005 - Score Report | ESPNcricinfo.com, he stood his ground for 53 deliveries, helping Michael Hussey push the Australian tail to a record tenth-wicket stand against South Africa of 107 runs.

- Glenn McGrath Personal life

Glenn's first wife, Jane Louise, was born in the United Kingdom and had worked as a flight attendant before their marriage. Glenn and Jane met at a Hong Kong nightclub called "Joe Bananas" in 1995, and married in 2001. They had two children, James and Holly. Jane McGrath fought recurrent battles with metastatic breast cancer, having been first diagnosed in 1997. On 26 January 2008 (Australia Day) Glenn and Jane McGrath were both made Members of the Order of Australia. Jane McGrath died, aged 42, on 22 June 2008 from complications following cancer surgery.

Glenn McGrath met Sara Leonardi, an interior designer, during the 2009 Indian Premier League. They married at home in Cronulla on 18 November 2010. In April 2011 McGrath put his home on the market for $6 million. Their daughter was born in September 2015.

In 2015 McGrath received widespread criticism when it was revealed he had killed a variety of animals during a hunting safari in South Africa. Photographs of McGrath appeared on the website of Chipitani Safaris, a game park, showing him crouched beside what looked to be a dead buffalo, two hyenas and the tusks of an elephant. He subsequently expressed his regret. McGrath had earlier told Australian Shooter magazine that "I'm keen to get into trophy hunting, no animal in particular, but a big safari in Africa would be great."

- Glenn McGrath McGrath Foundation

In 2002 Glenn and Jane founded the McGrath Foundation, a breast cancer support and education charity in Australia, which raises money to fund McGrath Breast Care Nurses in communities right across Australia and increase breast cancer awareness in young women. Since 2007, the third day of the first Test held in Sydney Cricket Ground is named Jane McGrath Day, even if the day is washed out. Following the death of Jane in June 2008, Glenn accepted the voluntary role of Chairman of the Board of the McGrath Foundation, and he participates in many activities in support of the Foundation to ensure the fulfilment of its vision. As of April 2016, the McGrath Foundation has placed 110 McGrath Breast Care Nurses around Australia, who have helped support more than 33,000 Australian families.

- Honours

1. In 2001, McGrath was one of just twenty-one Australian athletes inducted into the Australian Institute of Sport Best of the Best list.
2. He was awarded the Allan Border Medal and the Men's Test Player of the Year by CA in 2000. He was also awarded the Men's ODI Player of the Year in 2001.
3. McGrath was named a Member of the Order of Australia on 26 January (Australia Day) in 2008 for "service to cricket as a player", and along with his wife for "service to the community through the establishment of the McGrath Foundation." In 2008 McGrath was named the NSW Australian of the Year.
4. McGrath was inducted into the Sport Australia Hall of Fame in 2011, and the ICC Cricket Hall of Fame in January 2013. He was also inducted into the Australian Hall of Fame by the CA in 2013.
5. He was named as a bowler in Australia's "greatest ever ODI team." In a fan poll conducted by the CA in 2017, he was named in the country's best Ashes XI in the last 40 years.
6. A statue of McGrath by artist Brett "Mon" Garling was installed at McGrath's home town of Narromine in 2009.

- Records

1. McGrath was twice involved in tenth wicket partnerships which added 100 runs or more, a record matched only by New Zealand batsman Nathan Astle.
2. At the time of his retirement, McGrath's 7 for 15 against Namibia were the best bowling figures in a World Cup match, and the second-best in all ODIs. He also held the record for the most wickets in an edition of the

World Cup (26 in 2007) until this was broken by Mitchell Starc in 2019.

3. After his dismissal for a duck in the fourth test of the 2006–2007 Ashes series, McGrath claimed the record of having scored more ducks in Test cricket than any other Australian cricketer (35 – one more than Shane Warne).
4. McGrath holds the record for dismissing the most batsmen for ducks in Test cricket (104).

CHAPTER TWO

Australian Cricket history

- Australian Cricket history

Australian Cricket has a history spanning over 200 years. The earliest reports of the sport in Australia appeared in the Sydney Gazette - the first newspaper printed in the country in 1804 - and by 1826 there were records of clubs being formed in Sydney.

By 1832, clubs were forming in Tasmania; known at the time as Van Diemen's Land. In Western Australia, there is a record of labourers and mechanics taking on the builders of the new Government House as far back as 1835. The Melbourne Cricket Club was formed in 1838, and South Australia was participating in club cricket by 1839. From east to west, the sport was beginning to animate all corners of the nation.

In 1851, Victorians travelled to Tasmania to play the first intercolonial match, with 15,000 spectators in attendance. Such matches were known as Intercolonial matches until Federation in 1901, when they became Interstate matches.

1. The burgeoning sport required administration, with Boards of Control formed in New South Wales in 1857, Victoria in 1864 and South Australia in 1871.
2. There were tours of Australia by English sides in the summers of 1861/62 and 1863/64 before a team of Indigenous Australians became the first side to make a reciprocal tour to the northern hemisphere in the summer of 1868. That tour was led by Charles Lawrence, an Englishman who was part of the 1861/62 tour to Australia. He liked the country so much, he decided to stay.

3. Another English side – including the most famous player of the era, Dr W G Grace – toured Australia in 1873/74 before, in 1876/77, a combined New South Wales and Victorian side took on a touring English team at the Melbourne Cricket Ground for what became recognised as the first Test match. The Australians won by 45 runs and the match included an innings of 165 "not out" by the home side's Charles Bannerman, the first individual three-figure score in Test history.
4. An Australian side toured England in 1878 but the first Test match there did not occur until 1880 when the two sides met at The Oval in London. In 1882, after Australia's first victory on English soil, the legend of The Ashes – the mythical trophy that the two countries compete for in Test match cricket – began.
5. The Sheffield Shield domestic competition in Australia was initiated in 1892 by the Australasian Cricket Council, the first attempt at a national governing body. The Shield was the result of a donation by Lord Sheffield, the financier of an England tour of Australia in 1891/92.

As for the Council, it featured representatives of New South Wales, Victoria and South Australia with the aim of regulating Intercolonial cricket and organising international tours.

That latter role was one the players resisted, as private tours were a means for them to earn a living by playing the game. Indeed, in 1912, six of Australia's leading players - Warwick Armstrong, Vernon Ransford, Victor Trumper, Tibby Cotter, Hanson Carter and Clem Hill - all declined to tour England for a triangular tournament that also involved South Africa.

The public motive for their disquiet was that their choice of team manager had been rejected by the Australian Board of Control for International Cricket – the body formed in 1905 to replace the Australasian Cricket Council, which had been disbanded in 1899. But the underlying reason was the question of who should have access to the funds raised by such tours.

The trip took place without what became known as "The Big Six" and the control of the game by administrators over players became established. Armstrong would later go on to captain Australia to its first-ever clean-sweep of an Ashes series, a 5-0 success against a war-ravaged England team in 1920/21. That victory was spearheaded by fast bowlers Jack Gregory and Ted McDonald, establishing another principle in cricket that was to stand the test of time – whichever side had the best pace bowlers was more likely to prevail.

- The Meeting

The first meeting of the Australian Board of Control for International Cricket featured two representatives from each of New South Wales and Victoria. For its second meeting one delegate from Queensland was permitted to attend, and in 1906, three representatives of New South Wales, South Australia and Victoria plus one Queenslander were present. Tasmania's first delegate attended in 1907 and six years later they were joined by a single Western Australia official.

In 1914 and 1974 respectively, Queensland and Western Australia increased their representation to two delegates. By 1973, the body had become the Australian Cricket Board. It stayed that way until 2003, when the game's national governing body became Cricket Australia.

- The Sheffield Shield

The Sheffield Shield was played between three states – New South Wales, South Australia and Victoria – from its inception in 1892 until 1926/27, when Queensland joined. Western Australia was admitted in 1947/48 and Tasmania became the sixth state to play in the competition in 1977/78. Matches were timeless up to 1926/27, before becoming four-day contests. From 1982/83 the top two sides in the competition each season have played off in a final.

The first domestic one-day competition took place in the summer of 1969/70, although New Zealand competed until 1974/75, claiming victory three times. The Australian Capital Territory (ACT) had a side compete for three seasons from 1997/98.

- domestic Twenty20 tournament

A domestic Twenty20 tournament started in 2005/06. For its first six seasons, the competition was state-based before it was replaced by the Big Bash League in 2011/12 featuring eight teams; two each from New South Wales and Victoria plus one from Adelaide, Perth, Brisbane and Hobart. Unlike several other Twenty20 competitions around the world, Cricket Australia - as the governing body - retained overall control of the teams.

- Women Cricket After Progress

The history of women in cricket can be traced back to 1894, when a Tasmanian created the first local women's competition in Australia's history books. In 1931, the Australian Women's Cricket Association would form, with the Australian women's team taking to the world stage against England in 1934 in the first ever Test match. From Ruby Monaghan to Ellyse Perry. From grassroots to elite. This is the evolution of women's cricket in Australia.

Women's cricket in Australia is believed to have started in 1894 when a Tasmanian, Lily Poulett-Harris, created a local competition. Just over a decade later, in 1905, the Victorian Women's Cricket Association was formed, followed by the Australian Women's Cricket Association in 1931.

During the summer of 1930/31, the first Australian Women's National Cricket Championships (WNCC) took place. Three years, later women's international cricket was born when the Australian Women's Cricket Council invited the Women's Cricket Association of England to send a team on tour. That trip featured 14 three-day matches and included the first-ever Women's Test match.

From 1972/73, Australian domestic teams have taken part in the WNCC and play for the Ruth Preddey Cup, named after the former New South Wales player and journalist who helped to organize finance for a tour of England herself. A women's Twenty20 Cup was first played at national level in 2008/09, although the Australian Capital Territory and Tasmania were not admitted until the following summer.

The governing body for the women's game then merged with Cricket Australia in 2003, ensuring that the men's and women's sport was run by one single and unified body. That body formed the Women's Big Bash League; a domestic Twenty20 competition featuring the same sides as the men's short-form tournament in 2015.

- Today Women Cricket

In 2018, a record breaking 1,558,821 Australians actively engaged in cricket competitions or programs across the nation; an increase on nine per cent from the previous year. Six in every 10 new participants were females, and multicultural participation rose by four per cent, making up 22 per cent of all participants. Indigenous participation is also on the rise, with an increased participation level of one per cent.

CHAPTER THREE

Australia National Cricket Team

- Australia National Cricket Team

The Australia men's national cricket team represents Australia in men's international cricket. As the joint oldest team in Test cricket history, playing in the first ever Test match in 1877, the team also plays One-Day International (ODI) and Twenty20 International (T20I) cricket, participating in both the first ODI, against England in the 1970–71 season and the first T20I, against New Zealand in the 2004–05 season, winning both games. The team draws its players from teams playing in the Australian domestic competitions – the Sheffield Shield, the Australian domestic limited-overs cricket tournament and the Big Bash League.

The national team has played 837 Test matches, winning 397, losing 226, drawing 212 and tying 2. As of January 2021, Australia is ranked third in the ICC Test Championship on 113 rating points. Australia is the most successful team in Test cricket history, in terms of overall wins, win-loss ratio and wins percentage.

Test rivalries include The Ashes (with England), The Border-Gavaskar Trophy (with India), the Frank Worrell Trophy (with the West Indies), the Trans-Tasman Trophy (with New Zealand), and with South Africa.

The team has played 958 ODI matches, winning 581, losing 334, tying 9 and with 34 ending in a no-result. As of January 2021, Australia is ranked fourth in the ICC ODI Championship on 111 rating points, though have been ranked first for 141 of 185 months since its introduction in 2002.

Australia is the most successful team in ODI cricket history, winning more than 60 per cent of their matches, with a record seven World Cup final appearances (1975, 1987, 1996, 1999, 2003, 2007 and 2015) and have won the World Cup a record five times: 1987, 1999, 2003, 2007 and 2015. Australia is the first (and only) team to appear in four consecutive World Cup finals (1996, 1999, 2003 and 2007), surpassing the old record of three consecutive World Cup appearances by the West Indies (1975, 1979 and 1983) and the first and only team to win 3 consecutive World Cups (1999, 2003 and 2007). The team was undefeated in 34 consecutive World Cup matches until the 2011 Cricket World Cup where Pakistan beat them by 4 wickets in the Group stage.

It is also the second team to win a World Cup (2015) on home soil, after India (2011). Australia have also won the ICC Champions Trophy twice (2006 and 2009) making them the first and the only team to become back to back winners in the Champions Trophy tournaments. As of 2021, Australia is the only team to win five Cricket World Cups; no other team has won more than two.

The national team has played 153 Twenty20 International matches, winning 79, losing 69, tying 2 and with 3 ending in a no-result. As of November 2021, Australia is ranked sixth in the ICC T20I Championship on 246 rating points. Australia are the reigning ICC Men's T20 World Cup champions, defeating New Zealand in the 2021 final to claim their first T20 World Cup title.

On 12 January 2019, Australia won the first ODI against India at the Sydney Cricket Ground by 34 runs, to record their 1,000th win in international cricket.

- Australian cricket from 1876–77 to 1890

The Australian team that toured England in 1878

The Australian cricket team participated in the first Test match at the MCG in 1877, defeating an English team by 45 runs, with Charles Bannerman making the first Test century, a score of 165 retired hurt.Test cricket, which only occurred between Australia and England at the time, was limited by the long distance between the two countries, which would take several months by sea. Despite Australia's much smaller population, the team was very competitive in early games, producing stars such as Jack Blackham, Billy Murdoch, Fred "The Demon" Spofforth, George Bonnor, Percy McDonnell, George Giffen and Charles "The Terror" Turner. Most cricketers at the time were either from New South Wales or Victoria, with the notable exception of George Giffen, the star South Australian all-rounder.

A highlight of Australia's early history was the 1882 Test match against England at The Oval. In this match, Fred Spofforth took 7/44 in the game's fourth innings to save the match by preventing England from making their 85-run target. After this match The Sporting Times, a major newspaper in London at the time, printed a mock obituary in which the death of English cricket was proclaimed and the announcement made that "the body was cremated and the ashes taken to Australia." This was the start of the famous Ashes series in which Australia and England play a series of Test matches to decide the holder of the Ashes. To this day, the contest is one of the fiercest rivalries in sport.

- Golden age

History of Australian cricket from 1890–91 to 1900 and History of Australian cricket from 1900–01 to 1918

The so-called 'Golden Age' of Australian Test cricket occurred around the end of the 19th century and the beginning of the 20th century, with the team under the captaincy of Joe Darling, Monty Noble and Clem Hill winning eight of ten tours. It is considered to have lasted from the 1897–98 English tour of Australia and the 1910–11 South African tour of Australia. Outstanding batsmen such as Joe Darling, Clem Hill, Reggie Duff, Syd Gregory, Warren Bardsley and Victor Trumper, brilliant all-rounders including Monty Noble, George Giffen, Harry Trott and Warwick Armstrong and excellent bowlers including Ernie Jones, Hugh Trumble, Tibby Cotter, Bill Howell, Jack Saunders and Bill Whitty, all helped Australia to become the dominant cricketing nation for most of this period.

Victor Trumper became one of Australia's first sporting heroes, and was widely considered Australia's greatest batsman before Bradman and one of the most popular players. He played a record (at the time) number of Tests at 49 and scored 3163 (another record) runs at a high for the time average of 39.04. His early death in 1915 at the age of 37 from kidney disease caused national mourning. The Wisden Cricketers' Almanack, in its obituary for him, called him Australia's greatest batsman: "Of all the great Australian batsmen Victor Trumper was by general consent the best and most brilliant."

The years leading up to the start of World War I were marred by conflict between the players, led by Clem Hill, Victor Trumper and Frank Laver, the Australian Board of Control for International Cricket, led by Peter McAlister, who was attempting to gain more control of tours from the players. This led to six leading players (the so-called "Big Six") walking out on the 1912 Triangular Tournament in England, with Australia fielding what was generally considered a second-rate side. This was the last series before the war, and no more cricket was played by Australia for eight years, with Tibby Cotter being killed in Palestine during the war.

- Australian cricket from 1918–19 to 1930

Test cricket resumed in the 1920/21 season in Australia with a touring English team, captained by Johnny Douglas losing all five Tests to Australia, captained by the "Big Ship" Warwick Armstrong. Several players from before the war, including Warwick Armstrong, Charlie Macartney, Charles Kelleway, Warren Bardsley and the wicket-keeper Sammy Carter, were instrumental in the team's success, as well as new players Herbie Collins, Jack Ryder, Bert Oldfield, the spinner Arthur Mailey and the so-called "twin destroyers" Jack Gregory and Ted McDonald. The team continued its success on the 1921 tour of England, winning three out of the five Tests in Warwick Armstrong's last series. The side was, on the whole, inconsistent in the latter half of the 1920s, losing its first home Ashes series since the 1911–12 season in 1928–29.

- Australian cricket from 1930–31 to 1945

The 1930 tour of England heralded a new age of success for the Australian team. The team, led by Bill Woodfull – the "Great Un-bowlable" – featured legends of the game including Bill Ponsford, Stan McCabe, Clarrie Grimmett and the young pair of Archie Jackson and Don Bradman. Bradman was the outstanding batsman of the series, scoring a record 974 runs, including one century, two double centuries and one triple century, a massive score of 334 at Leeds which including 309 runs in a day. Jackson died of tuberculosis at the age of 23 three years later, after playing eight Tests. The team was widely considered unstoppable, winning nine of its next ten Tests.

The 1932–33 England tour of Australia is considered one of the most infamous episodes of cricket, due to the England team's use of bodyline, where captain Douglas Jardine instructed his bowlers Bill Voce and Harold Larwood to bowl fast, short-pitched deliveries aimed at the bodies of the Australian batsmen. The tactic, although effective, was widely considered by Australian crowds as vicious and unsporting. Injuries to Bill Woodfull, who was struck over the heart, and Bert Oldfield, who received a fractured skull (although from a non-bodyline ball), exacerbated the situation, almost causing a full-scale riot from the 50 000 fans at the Adelaide Oval for the third Test.

The conflict almost escalated into a diplomatic incident between the two countries, as leading Australian political figures, including the Governor of South Australia, Alexander Hore-Ruthven, protested to their English counterparts. The series ended in a 4–1 win for England but the bodyline tactics used were banned the year after.

The Australian team put the result of this series behind them, winning their next tour of England in 1934. The team was led by Bill Woodfull on his final tour and was notably dominated by Ponsford and Bradman, who twice put on partnerships of over 380 runs, with Bradman once again scoring a triple-century at Leeds. The bowling was dominated by the spin pair of Bill O'Reilly and Clarrie Grimmett, who took 53 wickets between them, with O'Reilly twice taking seven-wicket hauls.

Sir Donald Bradman is widely considered the greatest batsman of all time. He dominated the sport from 1930 until his retirement in 1948, setting new records for the highest score in a Test innings (334 vs England at Headingley in 1930), the most runs (6996), the most centuries (29), the most double centuries and the highest Test and first-class batting averages. His record for the highest Test batting average – 99.94 – has never been beaten. It is almost 40 runs per innings above the next highest average. He would have finished with an average of over 100 runs per innings if he had not been dismissed for a duck in his last Test. He was knighted in 1949 for services to cricket. He is generally considered one of Australia's greatest sporting heroes.

Test cricket was again interrupted by war, with the last Test series in 1938 made notable by Len Hutton scoring a world record 364 for England, with Chuck Fleetwood-Smith conceding 298 runs in England's world record total of 7/903. Ross Gregory, a notable young batsman who played two Tests before the war, was killed in the war.

- Australian cricket from 1945–46 to 1960

The team continued its success after the end of the Second World War, with the first Test (also Australia's first against New Zealand) being played in the 1945–46 season against New Zealand. Australia was by far the most successful team of the 1940s, being undefeated throughout the decade, winning two Ashes series against England and its first Test series against India. The team capitalised on its ageing stars Bradman, Sid Barnes, Bill Brown and Lindsay Hassett while new talent, including Ian Johnson, Don Tallon, Arthur Morris, Neil Harvey, Bill Johnston and the fast bowling pair of Ray Lindwall and Keith Miller, who all made their debut in the latter half of the 1940s, and were to form the basis of the team for a good part of the next decade. The team that Don Bradman led to England in 1948 gained the moniker The Invincibles, after going through the tour without losing a single game.

Of 31 first-class games played during the tour, they won 23 and drew 8, including winning the five-match Test series 4–0, with one draw. The tour was particularly notable for the fourth Test of the series, in which Australia won by seven wickets chasing a target of 404, setting a new record for the highest run chase in Test cricket, with Arthur Morris and Bradman both scoring centuries, as well as for the final Test in the series, Bradman's last, where he finished with a duck in his last innings after needing only four runs to secure a career average of 100.

Australia was less successful in the 1950s, losing three consecutive Ashes series to England, including a horrendous 1956 Tour of England, where the 'spin twins' Laker and Lock destroyed Australia, taking 61 wickets between them, including Laker taking 19 wickets in the game (a first-class record) at Headingley, a game dubbed Laker's Match.

However, the team rebounded to win five consecutive series in the latter half of the 1950s, first under the leadership of Ian Johnson, then Ian Craig and Richie Benaud. The series against the West Indies in the 1960–61 season was notable for the Tied Test in the first game at the Gabba, which was the first in Test cricket. Australia ended up winning the series 2–1 after a hard-fought series that was praised for its excellent standards and sense of fair play. Stand-out players in that series as well as through the early part of the 1960s were Richie Benaud, who took a then-record number of wickets as a leg-spinner and who also captained Australia in 28 Tests, including 24 without defeat; Alan Davidson, who was a notable fast-bowler and also became the first player to take 10 wickets and make 100 runs in the same game in the first Test; Bob Simpson, who also later captained Australia for two different periods of time; Colin McDonald, the first-choice opening batsman for most of the 1950s and early '60s; Norm O'Neill, who made 181 in the Tied Test; Neil Harvey, towards the end of his long career; and Wally Grout, an excellent wicket-keeper who died at the age of 41.

- World Series Cricket and Restructuring

The Centenary Test was played in March 1977 at the MCG to celebrate 100 years since the first Test was played. Australia won the match by 45 runs, an identical result to the first Test match.

In May 1977, Kerry Packer announced he was organising a breakaway competition – World Series Cricket (WSC) – after the Australian Cricket Board (ACB) refused to accept Channel Nine's bid to gain exclusive television rights to Australia's Test matches in 1976. Packer secretly signed leading international cricketers to his competition, including 28 Australians. Almost all of the Australian Test team at the time were signed to WSC – notable exceptions including Gary Cosier, Geoff Dymock, Kim Hughes and Craig Serjeant – and the Australian selectors were forced to pick what was generally considered a third-rate team from players in the Sheffield Shield. Former player Bob Simpson, who had retired 10 years previously after a conflict with the board, was recalled at the age of 41 to captain Australia against India. Jeff Thomson was named deputy in a team that included seven debutants. Australia managed to win the series 3–2, mainly thanks to the batting of Simpson, who scored 539 runs, including two centuries; and the bowling of Wayne Clark, who took 28 wickets.

Australia lost the next series 3–1 against the West Indies, which was fielding a full strength team; and also lost the 1978–79 Ashes series 5–1, the team's worst Ashes result in Australia. Graham Yallop was named as captain for the Ashes, with Kim Hughes taking over for the 1979–80 tour of India. Rodney Hogg took 41 wickets in his debut series, an Australian record. WSC players returned to the team for the 1979–80 season after a settlement between the ACB and Kerry Packer. Greg Chappell was reinstated as captain.

The underarm bowling incident of 1981 occurred when, in an ODI against New Zealand, Greg Chappell instructed his brother Trevor to bowl an underarm delivery to New Zealand batsman Brian McKechnie, with New

Zealand needing a six to tie off the last ball. The aftermath of the incident soured political relations between Australia and New Zealand, with several leading political and cricketing figures calling it "unsportsmanlike" and "not in the spirit of cricket".

Australia continued its success up until the early 1980s, built around the Chappell brothers, Dennis Lillee, Jeff Thomson and Rod Marsh. The 1980s was a period of relative mediocrity after the turmoil caused by the Rebel Tours of South Africa and the subsequent retirement of several key players. The rebel tours were funded by the South African Cricket Board to compete against its national side, which had been banned—along with many other sports, including Olympic athletes—from competing internationally, due to the South African government's racist apartheid policies. Some of Australia's best players were poached: Graham Yallop, Carl Rackemann, Terry Alderman, Rodney Hogg, Kim Hughes, John Dyson, Greg Shipperd, Steve Rixon and Steve Smith amongst others. These players were handed three-year suspensions by the Australian Cricket Board which greatly weakened the player pool for the national sides, as most were either current representative players or on the verge of gaining honours.

- Australian cricket from 1985–86 to 2000

The so-called 'Golden Era' of Australian cricket occurred around the end of the 20th century and the beginning of the 21st century. This was a period in which Australian cricket recovered from the disruption caused by World Series Cricket to create arguably the strongest Test team in history.

Under the captaincy of Allan Border and the new fielding standards put in place by new coach Bob Simpson, the team was restructured and gradually rebuilt their cricketing stocks. Some of the rebel players returned to the national side after serving their suspensions, including Trevor Hohns, Carl Rackemann and Terry Alderman. During these lean years, it was the batsmen Border, David Boon, Dean Jones, the young Steve Waugh and the bowling feats of Alderman, Bruce Reid, Craig McDermott, Merv Hughes and to a lesser extent, Geoff Lawson who kept the Australian side afloat.

With the emergence of players such as Ian Healy, Mark Taylor, Geoff Marsh, Mark Waugh, and Greg Matthews in the late 1980s, Australia was on the way back from the doldrums. Winning the Ashes in 1989, the Australians got a roll on beating Pakistan, Sri Lanka and then followed it up with another Ashes win on home soil in 1991. The Australians went on to the West Indies and had their chances but ended up losing the series. However, they bounced back and beat the Indians in their next Test series. With the retirement of the champion but defensive, Allan Border, a new era of attacking cricket had begun under the leadership of firstly Mark Taylor and then Steve Waugh.

The 1990s and early 21st century were arguably Australia's most successful periods, unbeaten in all Ashes series played bar the famous 2005 series and achieving a hat-trick of World Cups. This success has been attributed to the restructuring of the team and system by Border, successive aggressive captains, and the effectiveness of several key players, most notably Glenn McGrath, Shane Warne, Justin Langer, Matthew Hayden, Steve Waugh, Adam Gilchrist, Michael Hussey and Ricky Ponting.

- Australian cricket from 2000–01

Following the 2006–07 Ashes series which Australia won 5 nil, Australia slipped in the rankings after the retirements of key players. In the 2013/14 Ashes series, Australia again defeated England 5 nil and climbed back to third in the ICC International Test rankings. In February/March 2014, Australia beat South Africa, the number 1 team in the world, 2–1 and overtook them to return to the top of the rankings. In 2015, Australia won the World Cup, losing just one game for the tournament.

As of December 2020, Australia are ranked first in the ICC Test Championship, fourth in the ICC ODI Championship and second in the ICC T20I Championship.

- 2018 Australian ball-tampering scandal

On 25 March 2018, during the third Test match against hosts South Africa; players Cameron Bancroft, Steve Smith, David Warner and the leadership group of the team were implicated in a ball tampering scandal. Smith and Bancroft admitted to conspiring to alter the condition of the ball by rubbing it with a piece of adhesive tape containing abrasive granules picked up from the ground (it was later revealed that sandpaper was used). Smith stated that the purpose was to gain an advantage by unlawfully changing the ball's surface in order to generate reverse swing.

Bancroft had been filmed tampering with the ball and after being informed he had been caught, he was seen to transfer a yellow object from a pocket to the inside front of his trousers to hide the evidence. Steve Smith and David Warner were stood down as captain and vice-captain during the third Test while head coach, Darren Lehmann was suspected to have assisted Cameron Bancroft to tamper the ball.

The ICC imposed a one-match ban and 100%-match-fee fine on Smith, while Bancroft was fined 75 per cent of his match fee and received 3 demerit points. Smith and Warner were both stripped of their captaincy roles by Cricket Australia and sent home from the tour (along with Bancroft). Tim Paine was appointed as captain for the fourth Test. Cricket Australia then suspended Smith and Warner from playing for 12 months and Bancroft for 9 months. Smith and Bancroft could not be considered for leadership roles for 12 months after the suspension, while Warner is banned from leadership of any Cricket Australia team for life.

In the aftermath of these events, Darren Lehmann announced his resignation as head coach at the end of the series with Justin Langer replacing him. On 8 May 2018, Tim Paine was also named as the ODI captain while Aaron Finch was reinstated as T20I captain hours later, although Finch replaced Paine as the ODI captain after the 5-0 ODI series whitewash in England in June 2018.

On 7 October 2018, Australia played their first Test match under new coach Justin Langer and a new leadership group, which included Tim Paine as Australia's 46th Test captain. After a 1–0 loss to Pakistan in a two match Test series against Pakistan in the UAE and a 2–1 defeat against India in a four match Test series, they found success against Sri Lanka, winning the two Test match series 2–0.

In 2019, Australia played in the Cricket World Cup, where they finished second in the group stage before being knocked out by England at Edgbaston in the semi-final. Australia went on to retain the Ashes during the 2019 Ashes series, the first time on English soil since 2001, by winning the fourth Test at Old Trafford.

In 2020–21, Australia hosted India for 3 ODIs, 3 T20Is, and 4 Tests. They won the ODI series 2–1, but lost the T20I series 2–1. Then, the two teams competed for the Border-Gavaskar Trophy which saw one of the greatest overseas Test triumphs by India in the 4th Test to win the series 2–1 with the 3rd Test being drawn.

- Team colours

For Test matches, the team wears Cricket Whites, with an optional sweater or sweater-vest with a green and gold V-neck for use in cold weather. The sponsor's (currently Alinta for home matches and Qantas for away matches) logo is displayed on the right side of the chest while the Cricket Australia emblem is displayed on the left. If the sweater is being worn the Cricket Australia emblem is displayed under the V-neck and the sponsor's logo is again displayed on the right side of the chest. The baggy green, the Australian Test cricket cap, is considered an essential part of the cricketing uniform and as a symbol of the national team, with new players being presented with one upon their selection in the team. The cap and the helmet both prominently display the Australian cricketing coat-of-arms instead of the Cricket Australia emblem. At the end of 2011, ASICS was named the manufacturer of the whites and limited over uniforms from Adidas, with the ASICS logo being displayed on the shirt and pants. Players may choose any manufacturer for their other gear (bat, pads, shoes, gloves, etc.).

In One Day International (ODI) cricket and Twenty20 International cricket, the team wears uniforms usually coloured green and gold, the national colours of Australia. There has been a variety of different styles and layouts used in both forms of the limited-overs game, with coloured clothing (sometimes known as "pyjamas") being introduced for World Series Cricket in the late 1970s. The Alinta or Qantas logo is prominently displayed on the shirts and other gears. The current home ODI kit consists of green as the primary colour and gold as the secondary colour. The away kit is the opposite of the home kit with gold as the primary colour and green as the secondary colour. The home Twenty20 kit consists of black with the natural colours of Australia, green and gold strips. However, since Australia beat New Zealand at the MCG in the 2015 Cricket World Cup wearing the gold uniform, it has also become their primary colour, with the hats used being called 'floppy gold', formerly known as 'baggy gold', a limited-overs equivalent to a baggy green. Until the early 2000s and briefly in early 2020, in ODIs, Australia wore yellow helmets, before using green helmets as in test matches.

Former suppliers were Asics (1999), ISC (2000–2001), Fila (2002–2003) and Adidas (2004–2010) among others. Before Travelex, some of the former sponsors were Coca-Cola (1993–1998), Fly Emirates (1999) and Carlton & United Breweries (2000–2001).

- match records
- Team

1. Australia is the most successful Test team in cricketing history. It has won more than 350 Test matches at a rate of almost 47%. The next best performance is by South Africa at 37%.
2. Australia have been involved in the only two Tied Tests played. The first occurred in December 1960, against the West Indies in Brisbane.The second occurred in September 1986, against India in Madras (Chennai).
3. Australia's largest victory in a Test match came on 24 February 2002. Australia defeated South Africa by an innings and 360 runs in Johannesburg.
4. Australia holds the record for the most consecutive wins with 16. This has been achieved twice; from October 1999 to February 2001 and from December 2005 to January 2008.
5. Australia shares the record for the most consecutive series victories winning 9 series from October 2005 to June 2008. This record is shared with England.
6. Australia's highest total in a Test match innings was recorded in Kingston, Jamaica against the West Indies in June 1955. Australia posted 758/8 in their first innings, with five players scoring a century.
7. Australia's lowest total in a Test match innings was recorded in Birmingham against England in May 1902. Australia were bowled all out for 36.
8. Australia are the only team to have lost a Test match after enforcing the follow-on, having been the losing side in all three such matches
9. The first Test in the 1894–95 Ashes.
10. The third Test of the 1981 Ashes.
11. The second Test in the 2000–01 Border-Gavaskar Trophy series against India.
12. Against India in March 2013, Australia became the first team in Test history to declare in their first innings and then lose by an innings.
13. In the 2013–14 Ashes series, Australia took all 100 wickets on offer in the 5–0 sweep over England.
14. Ricky Ponting and Steve Waugh have played in the most Test matches for Australia, both playing in 168 matches.

- Batting

1. Charles Bannerman faced the first ball in Test cricket, scored the first runs in Test cricket and also scored the first Test century.
2. Charles Bannerman also scored 67.34% of the Australian first innings total in match 1. This record remains to this day as the highest percentage of a completed innings total that has been scored by a single batsman.
3. Ricky Ponting has scored the most runs for Australia in Test cricket with 13,378 runs. Allan Border is second with 11,174 runs in 265 innings a record which was broken by Brian Lara during his innings of 226 against Australia while Steve Waugh has 10,927 in 260 innings.Allan Border was the first Australian batsman to pass 10,000 and the first ever batsman to pass 11,000 Test runs.Ricky Ponting was the first Australian batsman to pass 12,000 and 13,000 Test runs.
4. Matthew Hayden holds the record for the most runs in a single innings by an Australian with 380 in the first Test against Zimbabwe in Perth in October 2003.
5. Donald Bradman holds the record for the highest average by an Australian (or any other) cricketer of 99.94 runs per dismissal. Bradman played 52 Tests, scoring 29 centuries and a further 13 fifties.
6. Ricky Ponting holds the record for the most centuries by an Australian cricketer with 41. Former Australian captain Steve Waugh is in second position with 32 centuries from 260 innings.
7. Allan Border holds the record for the most fifties by an Australian cricketer with 63 in 265 innings.
8. Adam Gilchrist holds the record for the fastest century by an Australian.
9. Glenn McGrath holds the record for the most ducks by an Australian cricketer with 35 in 138 innings.

- Bowling

1. Billy Midwinter picked up the first five-wicket haul in a Test innings in match 1.
2. Fred Spofforth performed Test cricket's first hat-trick by dismissing Vernon Royle, Francis McKinnon and Tom Emmett in successive balls.
3. Fred Spofforth also took the first 10-wicket match haul in Test cricket.

4. Shane Warne holds the record for the most wickets by an Australian cricketer with 708 wickets in 145 Test matches.
5. Arthur Mailey holds the record for the best bowling figures in an innings by an Australian cricketer with 9/121 against England in February 1921.
6. Bob Massie holds the record for the best bowling figures in a match by an Australian cricketer with 16/137 against England in June 1972. That was also his first Test match for Australia.
7. J. J. Ferris holds the record for the best bowling average by an Australian bowler, taking 61 wickets at 12.70 in his career.
8. Clarrie Grimmett holds the record for the most wickets in a Test series with 44 against South Africa in 1935–36.

- Fielding and wicketkeeping

1. Ricky Ponting holds the record for the most catches in a career by an Australian fielder with 196 in 168 matches.
2. Jack Blackham performed the first stumping in Test cricket in match 1.
3. Adam Gilchrist holds the record for the most dismissals in a career by an Australian wicketkeeper with 416 in 96 matches.

- Team

1. Australia's highest total in a One-Day International innings is 434/4, scored off 50 overs against South Africa in Johannesburg on 12 March 2006. This was a world record score before the South Africans later surpassed it in the same match.
2. Australia's lowest total in a One-Day International innings is 70. This score has occurred twice; once against England in 1977 and once against New Zealand in 1986.
3. Australia's largest victory in One-Day International cricket is 275 runs. This occurred against Afghanistan at the 2015 World Cup in Australia.
4. Australia are the only team in the history of the World Cup to win 3 consecutive tournaments; 1999, 2003 and 2007.
5. Australia went undefeated at the World Cup for a record 34 consecutive matches. After being defeated by Pakistan in 1999, Australia would remain unbeaten until they were again defeated by Pakistan in 2011.
6. Australia have won the most World Cups – 5.

Printed by Libri Plureos GmbH in Hamburg,
Germany